My Prodigal Journey

The journey away from the father's house is easier than the journey back home

Stephen Walley
Gene Walley
Virginia Walley

Instantpublisher.com

ISBN: 1-59196-571-3

My Prodigal Journey
The journey away from the father house is easier than the journey back home

Acknowledgements

The purpose of this book is to reflect on the experience of a modern prodigal and to present the grace and love of God to chase, chasten, correct, sustain and restore. My personal prodigal experience involved an extramarital affair, divorce, remarriage, and an abandoned ministry. What follows is an inside view from a prodigals perspective and that of his parents.

I am indebted to several people for what they have done in my life and helping with this book. To my wife who has experienced her own chastening and has found her own grace through this experience and who has chosen to make this marriage work against all odds. To my parents who have been totally honest, transparent, and loving. To those who have come along side of me and the ministry of Servants Alive by offering themselves and their resources; I am grateful for your friendship. We owe a great deal to our friend, Dr. Tom Whatley, for the encouragement, insight, and advice that he provided in the writing of this book. Thanks to Lisa Camp, she also helped with the editing and checking of grammar. To all who have tolerated me in the countless hours of writing, I say to you, "Thank You."

My Prodigal Journey

Reflections

1

The Sun is bright, expectations are high, seminary is completed and a new full time church waits. I come from good stock. My grandparents and parents were life long Baptist. I accepted Christ in my childhood, embraced the call to ministry in my late teens, and from a parent's perspective had a problem free childhood. No drugs, alcohol, smoking or sex. No continual late night adventures of wondering where I was.

Looking Back

When my mother was pregnant with me she was hospitalized with severe medical complications. The attending physician advised that the pregnancy should be terminated. This caused my folks a great deal of personal and theological issues. Our family physician was also a deep personal friend. He came by the hospital to see her as a friend, not as physician. Upon being told of their plight, our physician offered his advice; he suggested that my mother continue with the pregnancy and he even offered to take her case. When the attending physician was told that they wanted to proceed with the pregnancy, he became irate and told my parents that "if there was anything in there it would never be anything but an idiot." True enough there were many troubles ahead in the pregnancy and upon delivery the new physician told my parents, "The Lord must have some reason for this child for he should not have made it." Across the years when I would visit his office he would always tell me that God had a special purpose for my life.

My parents were ministers with my father in the full time pastorate my entire childhood. I entered college; my sophomore year I became engaged and I married my junior year. Forest Hills Baptist Church in Florence, Alabama, licensed me to preach at age 19 and Navco Baptist Church in Mobile, Alabama, ordained me at age 21; from the outside looking in some might have given two thumbs up. In fact, several did.

Upon completion of school I moved immediately into a full time church. Opportunities for service came quickly as well. Speaking and teaching engagements came frequently. In denominational work the places of service grew as well. I served on numerous committees at the local level and also had a position at the state level on the State Board of Missions. It was not uncommon for there to be several inquiries a month from churches looking to find a pastor both from inside the state as well as outside. I was young, I came from a pastor's home, and I had the academic requirements; "Flagship" was a word used by some when they talked about my potential in ministry.

The History Lesson

In time, what seemed bright and promising would become carnage of hurt, shame, and lost opportunities. How could one fall so far? How could one fall so fast? The answer was a heart unguarded. Many taught about how to protect your reputation and rightly so. The more critical issue was how do you protect your heart? The biblical writer says "Above all else, guard your heart, for it is the wellspring of life."[1]

History has it that the biblical city of Sardis was once captured for not guarding all of its sides. It seems that Sardis was built on cliffs. The invincibility of the cliffs led the city leaders to the conclusion it only needed to be guarded on one side. No need to worry about any attacks from the cliffs. Guess where the attack came? The cliffs! An army came to lay siege to Sardis and while staring up at the cliffs watched as a Sardine soldier (I guess that is what you called them.) leaned over the cliffs to observe the army below. The soldier's helmet fell all the way to the bottom and the siege army watched as the soldier descended the private trails to the bottom to retrieve the head gear. Under the cover of darkness, the army ascended the trails up the unguarded flank and took the city. All of this occurred because one side was left unguarded

A heart that was left unguarded would soon be unbridled. Layer upon layer of unhindered thoughts and fantasies corroded, corrupted, and eventually collapsed the heart. A corroded heart blinds eyes and set in motion a selfishness that became a recipe for implosion.

The journey from respected promising pastor to unfaithful husband and father was one that cannot be imagined. How does one describe completely the devastation brought to a wife, children, parents, family and friends, not to mention a church? What words would clearly paint a picture of the scars that run through the lives of those punctured by the sword of the prodigal?

Sermon after sermon and conference after conference declared the warnings of moral failure. As a child growing up the warning siren of moral failure was sounded. In the years of my parents being in the ministry there had been many of their contemporaries who experienced moral failure. Without exception it had proved to be devastating to each of them. Some of them had lost their families, and all had lost their ministries and disappeared into oblivion. They stood as an example of the high price to be paid for such behavior. There was such a powerful stigma attached to them for the rest of their lives.

In college the siren was sounded. In the seminary chapel, the siren was sounded. Among pastor friends in conversation the siren was sounded. Funny thing about the siren; I figured it must be sounding for someone else. Me? Not Me! I'm better than that. I'm smarter than that. I've got too much going for me to have that happen. I've got so much insulation. Pity the poor souls who have that happen to them; but not me. The siren sounds but it surely is not for me. The Bible clearly states "So, if you think you are standing firm, be careful that you don't fall![2] Pride goes before destruction, a haughty spirit before a fall."[3] While I'm unsure that the biblical writer was speaking specifically of moral failure the principal is clear; listen to the siren because it applies to you in every area.

The Soil

To understand the journey one must first understand the

ÄÄÄÄÄÄÄÄ

Above all else guard your heart for it is the wellspring of
life.

ÄÄÄÄÄÄÄÄ

soil from which the journey begins. The soil was not responsible for the trip but one must have a firm understanding of how the fertility of the soil relates to the ultimate outcome. Satan looks for fertile ground to sow his seeds. I do not think it matters to him how he neutralizes you to kingdom causes. It does not matter to him if it is through immorality, alcohol, drug addiction or just plain laziness. Any is acceptable to him. I can speak to the seeds of immorality. He may sow the seed but it is a personal choice to let it take root.

The thought field is among the first places where the seeds are sown in the soil. Thoughts that are allowed to enter the mind and take up residence without a challenge will soon take over. They will eventually reveal themselves in outward ways and that usually occurs at the worst times.

Sight is another field. It seems that every where a man might look his eyes can be fed with opportunity for immorality. For sure when he watches TV, even channel surfing, he will be presented with scantily clad women. When he turns the pages open in most magazines and newspapers he will face advertisement designed to catch his eye and stir his hormones. Many billboards flash opportunity in front of him. Enticing women are used to promote restaurants, automobiles, and beverages; the seed is sown!

Much of the music is slanted in that direction. From country to rock, the lyrics promote images of immorality. Covers of CD's and tapes push the limits of decency. The internet is now an easy access for most combining both sight and sound. There is a constant bombardment in our society with sexual allurement.

Many who are now in pastoral positions grew up in safe, respected, and treasured environments. That is particularly true for those preachers who grew up in preachers' homes. There is the seeming shield that "a man of the cloth" has around him to ward off suspicion. Nothing bad is going to harm him. He has the persona of being invincible. If you were to jerk open his shirt you would find "S" tattooed on his chest. He is a proverbial Superman. There is nothing he cannot handle. He can deal with the most difficult of crises to the most delicate of personalities. Into this role he is introduced to endless encounters with people of the opposite sex who confide in him of the needs not being met in their own marriage. There is a thin line that exist' between helping them spiritually and "helping" them physically. Put all that alongside periods of time in any day where he doesn't have to account for his time and trouble is ahead.

Most who find their way into pastoral ministry will soon ride along on the ego trip our society and, in particular, Baptist culture often places a preacher on; it is almost like being God. There is the need to be needed. There is the rush of people wanting your advice on any matter. After all, there really is not much you don't know. There is the hero complex. Call me I can help. I can get you out of any situation and fix any problem. The truth is that any preacher or man is just a very short step from the prodigal life because of how little attention is paid to the soil and the seeds that are being sown.

The Truth

Nothing in my background could be blamed for the collapse, nothing in my family, nothing in my education, and nothing in any of my churches. I had a healthy and happy childhood. I was the fourth and final child in our nest with one sister and two brothers. Our home was filled with a lot of laughter and we were family. We stuck by each other. My brothers and I had a basement full of bicycles that we fixed and toyed around with. We often played pranks on each other. Like any other family we went on vacations that were special. Before my sister was married we drove on vacation from Alabama to California to see my Dad's brother and his family. We never lacked for anything and were raised in a Christian environment. We had a daily prayer time in our home that included reading the Bible. There was a huge white bible that we used and we always read the names of the missionaries who were having birthdays. One of the big things in our home on Saturday nights was watching Hee Haw and folding church bulletins for Sunday. Sunday nights were leftover's from Sunday dinner and watching Bonanza. We always were in churches that treated my parents and us with the utmost respect. Clearly I was never traumatized. I was not mistreated nor misled. I wish I could now say that at the time of my great failure I was "lost". I can't. To the contrary, I was and am very much "saved", very much biblically informed, and indwelt by the Spirit of God.

I can't even give Satan the credit. There are those who might suggest that Satan led me down the broad path of destruction; truthfully he may have pointed out the path but to take the first step and all the steps that followed was my choice. Isn't that what occurred with Eve? She wasn't forced to eat anything. She chose to! Eve saw something that she wanted and   thought that it would improve her already perfect life. She must have pondered how it would satisfy her desires. She obviously gave little thought to the warning that had been given. No thought was given to what the consequences would be. It sounds very similar to the scenario in my life; I saw something that I wanted and thought only about how it would improve an already good life. The perception was it would satisfy my desires but I paid little attention to the warnings and gave no thought to the consequences.

It certainly would be nice and easy to lay it all at the feet of others. Eve did. Adam did. So did I. I blamed my wife, my parents, the stress of my job, the one I was involved with and even my school for not preparing me to deal with such. Unfortunately, to commit sin involves making a choice that sits squarely and totally on the shoulders of the one deciding. True enough, once the choice is made a whole lot of blinding and binding goes on. The choice, though, is solely reserved for the one deciding.

There once was a television commercial that used to simply ask "What if?" What a powerful question. What if? We have all asked ourselves that question at some point. Some before a decision is made and some after a decision is made. Trust me. That question runs through a prodigal experience from start to finish. What if? Every juncture brought that question "What if"? Like a pinball in a pinball machine, the question always rolled around begging to be pondered, but it was never answered.

Dwelling on the question led to confusion and anxiety. Often times it led to depression. What if I had taken responsibility for my thought and feelings? What if we had been caught in the act? What if it had ended before divorce? What if I had gone back? What if things had been different? What if this had never happen? What if I had put the same energy into making the marriage work as I had into making it fail? What if my lover and I manage to get together later on? What if I end up alone? What if my life ended now? What if my children will have nothing to do with me later on? How do you separate feeling from reality? Or is feeling reality?

ŏŏŏŏŏŏŏŏ

What If? Like a pinball in a pinball machine the question always rolled around begging to be pondered but it was never answered.

ŏŏŏŏŏŏŏŏ

The Heart of a Prodigal

2

The Bible describes the heart of man this way "The heart is deceitful above all things and beyond cure. Who can understand it?"[4] These words are certainly a very clear and adequate summary of the heart of a prodigal. A prodigal is one whose heart was once soft, sensitive, caring, compassionate, and even committed. For sure there was a time in my life when others' needs were a top priority. It was the thing that would cause me to rearrange my schedule even if it meant missing a family vacation to be there for a funeral. I would climb out of bed at all hours of the night to go to the hospital to be with one in a medical crisis. Driving for hours to be with a family in trouble was second nature. Countless hours of being at the hospital while someone had major surgery was common place. The prodigal experience is reflective of a change.

The prodigal is one self absorbed individual. Gone are the concern and interest in the plight of others. Their struggles are just that: their struggles. Others are hurting? So what! Some are crushed by life events. Tragic, but it doesn't concern me. Their issues became my inconvenience. Everything in my prodigal life was about me: my wants'. . . my needs. . . my pleasure . . . my ambitions. . . my desires. The only thing that matters is self.

Among the earliest steps to the prodigal lifestyle is the step of learning to look in the mirror and seeing only me and then learning to look at others and still seeing only me.

The Chicken or the Egg?

So how does one become a prodigal? It was like the chicken and the egg. Which came first? Was it pride or was it a hard heart? Which led to the other? I'm sure there are those who would debate it but as one who has tasted both the chicken and the egg I vote for pride. It was pride that allowed me to ensure myself that there was nothing that I could not handle. What followed was a heart that refused to seek God and refused to listen to God. Did you catch that line: refused to listen to God!

In the parable of the prodigal son that Jesus told in Luke 15, one has to wonder if the young man had to go all the way to the pig pen. Could it have been that had he been willing to listen to reason that he could have turned around before he started smelling like swine and craving their food? Could he have turned around before he found himself in a strange place foreign to him? Could he have come back home before he realized that he did not have any real friends? Could he have saved every penny of his fine inheritance if only he had turned before he walked away from the father's house? Could he have saved himself and his family the trauma of hurt and uncertainty had he turned before he ever asked his father for what he thought he was entitled to? He could have turned at any point before but he didn't turn until he reached the bottom. The bright young man did not have to go as far as he went but pride led to a hard heart.

In my opinion the seeds for disaster had been planted for some time in my life. The refusal to listen to God and see clearly that he was telling the truth about what was on the inside was common place. The seeds of pride had hardened my heart!

Enter an attractive woman with a warm smile and the stage was set. Lust was the enemy of purity. It was the incessant quest for the forbidden. Lust was a desire to have something I don't need and to enjoy something that in reality I already had. It was an insult to the provisions that God has made for me.

Lust intertwines with fantasy. Fantasy could take me anywhere. It was limited only by the boundaries of the mind. Fantasy would take on differing venues. Sometimes it would be as seemingly innocent as fantasizing that she would look in my direction, or that she would be where I was going to be. Other times it would be completely sexual. What would it be like to hold her and have her?

Fantasy could be such a tidy sin. No one could see it. It was just me and my thoughts. Only God knows and does he know! Fantasy became instant replay. In the morning, during the day, and at night the fantasy was available for my entertainment pleasure.

¤¤¤¤¤¤¤¤

In the morning, during the day, and at night the fantasy was available for my entertainment pleasure.

¤¤¤¤¤¤¤¤

Fantasy would fuel my lust and then lead to flirting. Flirting was most often the first outward expression of my inward fantasy. In the early stage it was "picking" with no apparent intention revealed. It became time consuming as it was difficult to flirt from a distance. You had to be sure that you put yourself in proximity; go stand by her, get in line near her, sit nearby her, make fun of certain things she said or did, compliment her dress and perfume and so on. Flirting eroded all boundaries relative to safety. I would tell myself "I can handle this and it is not out of control." But clearly it was. Flirting was the last step before what was on the inside, fantasy, made its outward debut.

In my flirting I never considered the full range of consequences. I only presumed the desired response would be the one I received. In reality she could have responded in negative ways to my advances which obviously would have led to trouble. She could have responded by slapping my face and chewing me out, by giving me a lecture or telling others about the advances. Flirting never thought about any of those or other consequences.

Pandora's Box

What doors was I opening that I could not close? When advances were made it was the opening of Pandora's Box. Lines were crossed from which there was no room to escape. Human emotions are a fickle thing. The need to have feelings soothed and egos warmed was very great. The eruption of emotion flowed like fresh spring water. It was new. It was different. It was intoxicating. Feelings never intended became the rule of the day. What's more it was a two way street; emotions in me and emotions in her.

Forgotten in the moment were the sacred lines of marriage. The uniqueness of the emotional, spiritual, and physical bonds that marriage is designed to have and, in fact, demand is such that they must be protected at all cost. The walls that guard those areas were weakened by the weight of flirting. Lost was the response of those who will be affected by your choices as they discovered what was going on.

Before you can bat your eye you can be struck with the fire of emotional involvement. It swept over me like a prairie fire clouding my perspective and perception. In the short term it weakened my resolve and strengthened my desire. It left me parched with a thirst for more. It met me in the morning and walked with me through the day. It ran through my mind like electricity through a wire, invading even my dreams. The need was to see her, be around her, and hear her voice. All the while I stood boldly confident that I was in charge of my emotions and that it was not the other way around. Denial was starting to claim another victim. Fantasy was about to make flirting pay off.

What had been emotional became sexual. The distance was not that far. The illusion was that it compared to nothing else and no one else. A great deal of the sexual thrill in reality may not have been sexual at all. There was thrill in doing something that was wrong. There was the threat of being bold and daring and the sense of having gotten away with something that nobody knew about.

These played a sadistic role in the web that was being woven. It was the wonder of the chase, the anticipation of a response, the thrill of being sneaky and the smell of stupidity. It violated all common sense and common decency. It reduced the crowning act of Gods creation to animalistic behavior driven by emotion, hormones, and deception. The places I went, the chances I took, the things I did, and that which I threw away, were indescribable in terms of how repulsive they were to God and others.

The Dual Lifestyle

Being involved with someone was exhausting. There were reasons beyond the physical toll. The emotional and mental strain of knowing what I knew and playing games to keep others from knowing was draining me. The acting that went on in presenting my self as one thing when I had clearly become something different exacted my energy. Attempting to show my self to be an interested husband, a caring father, and a spiritual pastor continued the drain. The constant grind of the spiritual, mental, and physical were at times debilitating. Living in the air of suspicion was perilous. Every time someone asked for a private word with me my first thought was "what do they know?" Each ring of the phone I would ask that haunting question to myself "was it someone who might some how know about my relationship?" After each encounter, the worry that someone have seen or heard rushed to the front of my thoughts. My mind could not keep focus, my spirit was drying up and my physical energy was depleted.

The dual lifestyle was more than I was designed to endure. Trying to remember where I said was, what I said I was doing, and who I said I was with was a trap set to spring later. Numerous times the trap would spring and a couple of things would always be consistent when it did; it always happened when I least expected it and reacting to it only served to set more traps. It might be sprung by something I said, by an innocent question someone asked, or an appointment I was late for.

Something had to give and one area that seemed to have some flexibility was work. Things could be shifted around and some assignments passed along to others. Concentration, discipline, and fairness quickly disappeared. The lack of preparation and attention to details at work soon created tension among my co-workers.

The loss of credibility was much like beach erosion. I would not determine the extent of the damage until the storm is completely passed. At the time I was in no way concerned with credibility. The assumption was that either I would always have it or that I would never need it. Wrong on both counts! The credibility I once had was eaten away with each act of deception until I had none at all. The size of the hole created by its absence was incredible. There was no substitute for credibility. Each dishonest act was a separate chisel chiseling away at my personal credibility. Every act of deception was another chisel. Any structure can logically sustain only so much chiseling before total collapse occurs.

Damage Control

Damage control is an element of any disaster. It is an attempt by those in charge to limit how much damage is actually allowed to occur in the disaster. The same was true in the case of an unfaithful husband, father, and minister. Managing my guilt was absolutely essential. There were many scenes where guilt would come rushing in. Without the ability to manage my guilt I might do the rational thing and stop doing the very things that produced the guilt. Those scenes occurred at unsuspecting times and places. The look from an innocent child brought guilt and damage control. The sincere words of my spouse produce guilt and damage control. The faces of my congregational folk who were seemingly clueless to my behavior brought me guilt and damage control. The awareness of my responsibilities was a constant source of guilt and damage control. A look at my family album would bring it on. It became more and more apparent that I must learn to manage my guilt.

Someone has said that what separates this generation from all others is the ability to manage our guilt. Learning to lessen the impact of the conscience was important to the one who was being convicted by the Spirit of God. I learned not to dwell on the things that facilitated guilt and to focus on what I wanted. Things that would have made my grandparents blush became common place in my thoughts and actions.

Guilt that became managed soon lost its punch. Gone were the convicting thoughts. With it went the attempts to gain my attention. Gone were the opportunities to turn around before I got too far from the father's house. Gone were the opportunities to avoid impending disaster!

✠✠✠✠✠✠✠✠

Guilt that becomes managed will soon lose its punch.

✠✠✠✠✠✠✠✠

A Real Man and Real Risk

If you tried to define a real man many would define him as one who is responsible. What that means is he cares for his family; he keeps a good job and never jeopardizes their future. In a culture that has focused on giving our children a good education so their quality of life is at least potentially better than our own, the very thought of doing anything to damage that potential is mind boggling. Yet that is exactly what I did. I set about to deliberately put my children's well being and future at risk.

The loss of steady income put them at financial risk. I will never know the real depth of disadvantage that my children have had to endure. I do know that others have had to assist them. Particularly early on in the experience I was simply unable to financially provide as I should have. I am clueless to the total financial risk they were exposed to.

I also know that they were put at risk emotionally. Having to deal with the absence of a father is one thing. Having to deal with it in a small town where such embarrassing behavior was involved is another. When they went to their school, their church, or just about anywhere in their town, their friends and their friend's parents knew who they were and knew what their daddy had done. Children have a great deal of elastic and I am sure that my children had theirs stretched to the limits. Fortunately for them, their mother went to great lengths at the expense of a great deal of energy to provide them with a stable environment.

Perhaps saddest of all, the children were put at spiritual risk. How involved would they be in church? What kind of personal daily walk with the Lord would they have modeled for them and what encouragement would they receive to do so? Would bitterness and blame consume them? If so, for how long? What negative influences would be placed in their path?

All these questions I never bothered to ask and frankly my behavior indicated I really did not care. How can you say you care about your children the way a responsible Christian parent should when you are blatantly jeopardizing their future? If someone else had been doing these things to my children putting them at risk financially, emotionally, and spiritually, I would have gone ballistic. When did it become wrong for someone else to do it and okay for me to do it?

Maligned Ministry

Another area that reflected the prodigal heart is in the area of ministry. There was a place and time in my life when I wrestled with God over what He wanted me to do with my future. I played golf in high school and was fortunate enough to have some interest from schools relative to a scholarship. The thought of eventually becoming a professional golfer buzzed in my head as a teenager. The struggle to respond to the call of God for my life was no small one. It became harder and harder to deal with his convicting work in my life. I remember the great peace that came when I embraced the fact that God wanted to use my life for his purpose in his ministry.

All through school God made a way for me. He supplied all of my needs and gave me opportunities to lead in worship. I accepted my first church at age twenty one and I always had a place to preach. I always had good churches and my experiences were positive. God allowed me the respect of my peers and trusted me with great responsibilities. What I was able to experience and achieve were all an act of God's grace and care.

The prodigal heart quickly forgets that "...every good and perfect gift is from above...[5] Focus was lost and slothfulness set in. The urgency of the call of God wanes in the heart. Visits were not made. Calls were not returned. Studies were not carried out. Plans were not made. Preparation became a thing of the past. There was pure arrogance and stupidity by standing in a place of divine calling and treating it as a common thing! Fear of the Lord was lost. The assignment was wasted on selfishness.

How long can you function in your work without taking care of your business? In the case of ministry how far can you go and how can you survive using old material and failing to provide leadership? The answer is, not as far as you think! To study consistently requires self discipline. Study is hard work and requires focus and time. A good sermon has fifteen to twenty hours of preparation involved over several weeks. With a prodigal heart that discipline began to disappear. It did so for a several reasons. One was spiritual things gave way to the secular and another reason was the absolute loss of focus. It showed itself very early when I was not prepared and when I was absent in leadership.

How could I have complete disregard for the highest call and privilege a human being can have? The answer was a prodigal heart! It was clear that the anointing of God cannot be shared with adultery. Without the presence of the Lord on the ministry I performed, I became nothing more than "...a resounding gong or a clanging cymbal"[6] functioning in my own ingenuity and strength. My prodigal heart did not care that the power of God was absent. The longing for His presence was no longer sought.

24

Roadblocks

How many times have we traveled down a road only to find a road block? Often the road block is the form of a *Warning Road Closed* sign. You don't have to stop; you can challenge the sign, run through the sign, run around the sign, or ignore the sign. Drive far enough and fast enough and there will no longer be road blocks. All the warnings will be over and you are left with only you, the road, and whatever the road has for you. There are a lot of possibilities of what the road beyond the road block might be like. It could be the pavement has been removed and to drive on could result in your losing control of what you are driving, resulting in injuries. Perhaps the bridge is out and there is no detour. To continue to drive on would prove to be fatal. Proceeding around the roadblock is a picture of the pride that results in a hard heart.

I could not begin to count exactly how many road blocks I ran through. They came in various sizes and shapes. They appeared at different times of the day or night. The first roadblock that was run past was that of the call of the Holy Spirit. He repeatedly tried to warn me speaking to my conscience. What was once a whisper by the Spirit of God crescendo into a loud yell. Other roadblocks showed up in physical ways such as being nervous and my heart rate going up. Early on they continued with intensity to inform you of impending danger and the need to turn around now.

Each time the road block sign was bigger and brighter. Having tuned out listening to the road blocks of the inner man, God then moved to give outer signs. Whether it was someone who almost heard you, almost saw you, or almost caught you, the sign was there. Whether or not they knew was irrelevant. I knew. Another sign! Another road block ignored! Pride got stronger, the heart got harder, and total collapse got closer.

Just how hard my prodigal heart had become border lined on being unreal. The cold hearted crass approach to people I said I loved and cared about reeked with the odor of selfishness. The heart had hardened to the point that it no longer mattered that your wife, children, and parents are devastated and humiliated. Their pleas did not bother me. Their tears did not move me. Their pain did not stop me. Road block . . . Road block . . . Road block . . . Drive on . . . Drive on . . . Drive on.

With each road block there came a thin layer of resentment that anyone for any reason would try and interfere with my getting what I wanted. Over time the layers of resentment and bitterness became bigger and stronger. The size and depth alone would serve to prove there was no limitation to what the outcomes could be. The thin layers harden the heart with lost sensitivity and growing selfishness. The point was reached where I didn't care who is hurt or how badly. My prodigal heart beat only for the moment, living for now, and it was bent on fulfilling its desires for itself.

Layer by layer the heart became insulated from the sounds of reality and isolated from others. The game went on. I felt insulated and isolated. I was insulated to the still small voice of God. I was isolated from those who loved me. I naturally pushed them farther and farther away. While the game of being insulated and isolated continued, one thing had not changed. The prodigal in me was still tethered to the truth! The tether may be long, but at some point it will snap through the cold hard layers and the prodigal would stare reality in the face. Where were all those road blocks?

26

¤¤¤¤¤¤¤¤

Their pleas didn't bother me. Their tears did not move me. Their pain did not stop me.

¤¤¤¤¤¤¤¤

Reality

Prodigals find it hard to be around non-prodigals because of the clear reminder of what the prodigal is not. What the prodigal is not is *right*. The prodigal knows what the prodigal should be. The common response was to justify it by saying "I'm as good as they are." The insulation against reality was a deadly thing. While the prodigal is very clear on what the prodigal isn't, he does not have a clue as to what he is.

For me the hardened heart was a masterpiece of blaming and justifying. The process continued and the distortion of reality grew. The voice inside said "This can't be as wrong as they say it is," "Everyone else gets what they want." "No one will ever know." "Others are not being hurt by this." The reality was this prodigal was not only *doing* something but also had *become* something. The journey to satisfy myself was under way and I became more and more fixated on myself in order to keep up the quest.

The Old Testament will often show the dwelling place of God in the singular, ie the House of the Lord, the Temple of the Lord, or the Tabernacle of God. Contrast that with how the Old Testament often reflects on the dwelling place of the wicked in the plural. It speaks of the "tents" of the wicked, and the "houses" of the wicked. I take from

27

that contrast that the wicked must go from one unfulfilling experience to another unfulfilling experience, quite literally from one tent of wickedness to another tent of wickedness. Those who are willing to encounter God will find in one place and in one personality everything they need. My trip as a prodigal was from one unfulfilled experience to another. Being so absorbed with the pursuit of me, I didn't see or understand just how selfish I really was.

Convinced no one knew what was going on; I picked up the pace in the pursuit. Besides, how could anyone know anything? All the phone calls could not give it away. The change in personal attitude could not give it away. The change in personal behavior such as changes in your daily routine and the growing list of *almost caught* could not be sending anybody a message! The reality is they knew and He knew!

Parents Perspective

In years past life had been good; God had blessed. We had a great ministry and a great family. All was well and we were content and happy, pleased with ourselves and where we were. Another person's choices cut directly across our own, taking us where we never wanted to be. How could this be happening? Suddenly our world and our lives were in shambles. Would we ever be able to rise from the rubble? How could we face others?

The questions, the whispers, the rejection by our peers! All of those brought pain but most painful was the wound created by our own son. The wound was so deep, so gaping; it was almost fatal. There was no way that we could foresee or be prepared for what was ahead. The bewilderment, the anger, how could this child do this? The agony of watching your child, your flesh and blood, self destruct. What had we done wrong? How had we failed? Why are we to blame for this?

Most troublesome was the inability to reach out, relate, and talk to him. There had always been such a special and close relationship with this son. He was a special gift from God. Due to medical problems we were not supposed to have this child, but God had other plans. How could we be living such a disaster? We wanted to believe this was just a bad dream and when we awoke everything would be just right again. Unfortunately, it was not just a dream and it really was a disaster.

Hard Heart and Hard Head

3

How does it start? There are many ways to begin such a journey. In my opinion, there has to be two things in place. First, there must be in your mind a little something wrong in your marriage, regardless of how small. Second, there must be a whole lot wrong with you. It is amazing how you simply reverse them. There was nothing wrong with me and everything was wrong with this marriage. Now you can easily justify everything you do. Like all marriages mine was not perfect. In retrospect, the bigger issue, though, was what was wrong in me.

A simple look, a smile, or the smell of perfume may be the entrance to the senses that lead to the mind. The distortion of reality was so swift it made justifying all the easier. No one has ever been so concerned for me. Lie. No one has ever shown such interest in me. Lie. No one has smiled at me like that. Lie . . . lie . . . lie. All lies. I can recall buying into all three lies. In reality I would have heard them as lies. But we aren't dealing with reality.

My affair lasted a very long period of time. The tension between being involved with someone and trying to carry on a family began to take a toll. The signals were growing in number that things were going to have to change. Questions were starting to be asked and people were starting to talk. I had told my wife about the affair but lied by telling her it was over. One thing became very clear; I was going to have to make some decisions or others would start making decisions for me. The *others* could be my wife, the person I was involved with, other family members, or people in my church. Time was running out on my dual life.

¤¤¤¤¤¤¤

Time was running out on my dual life.

¤¤¤¤¤¤¤

Early Monday morning of October 25, 1993 I got out of bed and starting packing my belongings. I told my wife that I was leaving. She made her way to the kitchen and watched as I loaded my car as quickly as I could. Nervously I moved through the house carrying out clothes and personal belongings, trying to hurry and avoid a real confrontation. Every trip back through the door was done so wondering what she would say or do. She did tell me that she couldn't take much more of this. I don't know what she thought. I believe in her mind she was doing all she could to make things work. She wanted to believe that it would work but the pressure was building on her as well. She had heard this "I'm leaving" stuff before and now it was being told to her again. I would not be so presumptuous as to suggest that I could understand what she was feeling or thinking but I am confident that she sensed her world was coming apart to say the least.

Having loaded the car, I went in and woke up my oldest son and told him I was leaving. I wanted to really have a long clear talk with him but I did not want a scene. I wanted to avoid anything that might cause me to rethink what I was doing. I tried to tell him that it was not his fault and that I would always be his father. All this was heavy stuff for a child before seven a.m. I kissed him and the toddler goodbye and walked out of the door.

I left and rode to my office where I wrote out my resignation. Numbness engulfed me as I sat there putting pen to paper. Honestly, I don't remember what I wrote. While I was there, I informed my lover of what I had done and where I might go, but I was unclear of what she might do. The resignation was placed in my desk drawer and I walked out, leaving my library and other personal effects in the office. I would later call the chairman of the deacons to tell him where he could find my resignation so he could read it the coming Wednesday evening.

It is a two hour drive from my home to my parents' home. Dressed only in sweat pants, a pull over shirt, and a baseball cap, I started in that direction. The ride was filled with trying to find ways to preoccupy my mind and not think about what I was doing. I wanted to be strong and in control when I talked to my parents. My mind raced between wondering what was going on at my home to what was going on with my lover to what my parents might say or do.

More Broken Hearts

Shortly I knocked on the door at my parents' home. By this time it was mid morning and dad had made his way to his office. Mother opened the door with great surprise to see me. I asked if dad was home, and when she informed me he wasn't, I asked her to call him and have him come

34

home. She asked me if something was wrong, and I told her I just needed to talk to both of them. Again she asked if everything was okay, fear rising in her voice. I lied assuring her everyone was alright and she called dad's office. "You need to come home; Steve is here and he needs to talk to us." With the phone receiver placed firmly back in its place, the expression on her face was in agreement with every maternal instinct she possessed. "Steve, what is it?" I refused to reveal anything until dad came home. For sure her nerves were churning and her mind was racing.

Most likely she revisited a few weeks earlier when I had "left", driven to another part of the state, and immediately returned home. Other family members had told them of my leaving and they came to my house and were there when I came in. They learned then of the affair and I promised them that it was over.

Shortly the door opened and dad came in. He too had fear all over his face. "What is wrong?" I told the two of them to come over and sit down. With all of us seated, I began to inform them that I had decided to leave my wife and the boys and this time it was for good. "I love someone else. I don't know what she is going to do but I have made my decision and there is no going back." It was as though my parents melted into their seats like warm butter on a kitchen counter. There are no words to describe the feelings they had at that particular moment. They gasped for air as though all the oxygen had been sucked out of the room. "What do you mean?" The conversation moved back and forth and soon gave way to tears of sorrow and moans of grief on their part. For my part the jaw was set, the attitude arrogant, and the heart was cold and hard. Never at any point did I waver or consider reconsidering. They held me in their arms as though I was a new born lifted from its crib and cried, pleading with me to do the right thing.

What an indication of just how cold and cruel my heart had become. Nothing moved me. These were my parents! My mother had made personal sacrifices to work and help me go to school and have transportation. They had helped me with getting cars and taking care of other needs that arose across the seven years of being in school. Mother had often given me surprises of encouragement. My dad and I shared much in common. We were both in ministry and talked regularly about our respective responsibilities. We also loved to play golf and from the age of fifteen we had spent a lot of time together on the course. We played golf together sometimes weekly. Our families often traveled together to state and national meetings. Even as special as these relationships were, they proved no match for a hard heart. Parents who had poured their energy into making their baby boy a success were now greeted by their grown son whose heart was bent on self destruction and public humiliation.

¤¤¤¤¤¤¤¤

They gasped for air as though all the oxygen had been sucked out of the room.

¤¤¤¤¤¤¤¤

I pried my parent's fingers away from me and told them I would see them later. I jumped in my car and started backing out of the drive only to catch a glance of two people whose lives had just been pulverized. The looks on their faces were descriptions of shock and bewilderment. I did not want to have to deal again with the looks on those faces anytime soon. Fearing that on impulse they would try to follow me, I drove several back roads and doubled back several times like an old western rider ensuring I wasn't seen by them. It would be quite a while before we would speak again, leaving them to wonder where I was or if I was ok. I let them go to bed and experience nightmares each night. That Monday would be a day that would create a scar that they would have for the rest of their lives. It was further indication of a hard heart!

Running through Mid Night

Once I arrived in Montgomery, I checked into a hotel on the eastern side of town. I was unsure of what I would do next and I had no idea whether my lover and I would be together or not. I did not leave to be with her; I left because I knew I had to make my own choices before other people started making choices for me. A prodigal cannot stand for others to make his decisions! I wanted her to be with me, but I really did not know if she had the courage or desire to leave her family and home. I really had nothing to offer her. For sure, I would be starting over with basically the stuff in my car and the clothes on my back. Not much to offer someone who has an already secure lifestyle; I believed we cared for each other, but I was not convinced of what she would do. Her family was well-known and well-respected in our town. She had her own issues of children and parents who lived in close proximity to each other; she had a very nice home and deep roots.

Thinking that someone might have followed me I tried to hide my car by turning it where the tag could not be seen and putting it in a lot apart from the hotel. My mind was starting to think like a criminal on the run. Late in the afternoon I carefully started to my car, looking out into the parking lot to see if anyone was there. Before I realized it there was my lover circling around the lots with her car loaded with her personal items. I came up from behind her car as she slowly made her way around the lot and appeared in front of her from nowhere. Her eyes were swollen from having cried all the way to Montgomery. When I first glanced at her terror went through me. "Has

37

anybody followed you? I asked. "I don't know," she responded. The terror I felt came from the realization that for the first time in this affair *I knew* my family knew *and* her family knew. How would they react? Were we in fear of personal safety? How had her husband taken her news? How had my wife taken the news? Fear became a paralyzing factor in my life.

I instructed her to quickly hide her car and get her belongings and get inside the room. Once inside the room I grilled her again over what had happened as she told her family and what were their reactions? She described for me what she had told them and what they had told her. There was never any hint of personal threat but paranoia began to take over. When I told her of my fears she too became afraid. Later we would learn that family members had indeed set out to search and I am not sure what the results would have been had they located us. We spent several days holed up inside the hotel, afraid to venture out. I had even gone down to the desk to have the room placed under a different name so as not to be traced. Believe me when I say that those days were definitely not spent engaged in a love fest. In fact there was real oddity in that we were actually together spending all of our time with each other. After several days we decided to take one car and head north. Where we were going, we didn't know. It was time to move and so we did.

Neither of us called our families and we traveled north up through Georgia and Tennessee. I had leads on a job in Knoxville, so after a couple of days I connected with that company to find out what the possibilities were. I did not want to be that far from my children so I tried to figure out where my wife and children might go. Trying to consider what her options might be, I convinced myself that Montgomery would be the most sensible place for me to go. It was likely I would not be more than a couple of hours from any place that she might go. Living each day waiting for someone to pop up from around any corner was creating a great deal of paranoia. It also further hardened my heart to a coldness and stubbornness.

On one of my trips home to pick up a few more items, as I walked out the door to leave my oldest son placed a tight grip to my leg and with a sobbing red face squealed "Daddy please don't go". That would ordinarily make any sensitive caring dad do a double take. A wife through her tears saying "I really think we can work this out" would generally be enough to at least bring on further discussion. They just didn't understand who and what they were dealing with. Neither did I! A hard heart and a hard head was exactly what we were dealing with. For sure a lot of my recent life had been lived in the dark but what was ahead was an absolute running through midnight.

Looks and Pleas

What kind of person with any sense of care and responsibility wakes a wife and child from a cold deep sleep and tells both he is leaving? What kind of person tries to explain to a sleepy seven year old "It's not your fault" while he is packing his car with all he can put in the four doors and trunk? What kind of a person kisses both the seven year old and the toddler good bye in a mad rush to get into his car and leave? It is the portrait of a man out of control; so out of control that he goes by his office in the church and cowardly leaves his resignation in the desk drawer. He then notifies his lover that he has left and then drives two hours to inform his parents of his "decision."

How could you be so cruel and insensitive? Little did I realize that those looks and pleas would later return in a different form; a form that I wished I could get away from, but unknowingly they were sealed into my mind. They would show up in some of the oddest places. They would suddenly appear in the grocery store when a young mother with two small children passed you in the aisle. They would appear at a traffic light when you pulled beside

✿✿✿✿✿✿✿✿

my oldest son placed a tight grip to my leg and with a
sobbing red face squealed "Daddy please don't go." That
would ordinarily make any sensitive caring dad do a double
take.

✿✿✿✿✿✿✿✿

a car that held two occupants that resembled your parents.
It would sneak up on you at the post office when a small
child called for his "daddy". The sight of a car the same
color as the one your family had would bring out the
reminder of faces and pleas. There was no way to escape
their impact!

Cold Heart and Open Hand

Early one Saturday morning the door bell at the
apartment rang. By this time everyone knew that I was in
an apartment in Montgomery. I had gone out and purchased
new furniture to furnish it. We were living together and our
divorces were not yet finalized. I stared through the peep
hole to see my parents standing on the other side. I didn't
have a shirt on because we were still in the bed, sleeping in
on Saturday. For sure we were not expecting company.
Reluctantly I opened the door. I was greeted with words of
how much I was loved and missed.

Even with a cold heart I was so ashamed for my parents
to come and find me living with her while not married. The
last thing I wanted was for them to come in for a visit.
Most of all I could not stand their grace. I searched for a

way to get them out of my hair and when the comment was made that they "knew I was not happy living in the situation" that was the spark I needed. I exploded on my parent's right there in the foyer of the apartment. I talked to both of them in a threatening and disrespectful way. They melted with disappointment and hurt. I slammed the door in their faces telling them they were not coming into the apartment. I went inside to the kitchen window to watch two people climb into their car and drive away, grieving and sobbing openly. They must have felt that it would have been easier driving away from the graveside of their son than what they were going through. I stood unmoved, glad to be relieved of their pressure, and proud to have "put them in their place." Time to go back to bed!

I remember a time when I needed some money and I needed it fast. The financial walls were falling in and time was short. I felt that someone had to help me and the list was short for those who might even be willing. I made a call to my parents who were glad, and I suspect suspicious, of my making contact with them. After a brief exchange of pleasantries I informed them I needed some help to the tune of several thousand dollars. There was a silence for what seemed like a day. My parents informed me they wanted to help if they could, but they would have to see what they could do. The following day they called to set up a time when they would meet me. They had worked out the arrangements some way to get the money. We agreed to meet in the parking lot of the apartment complex the following morning. We sat in their car with them in the front seat and me in the back. There was a great deal of tension inside the sedan and little time was spent in getting straight to the point. The relief of knowing that I could take care of some pressing obligations was almost giddy.

With the money came having to listen to what they had to say. They were very strong about how they felt and wasted few words. They made it clear to me how they felt about my having left my former wife and sons, having abandoned the ministry, and where I was now. With the exchange of the money I told them thank you in a very polite way and then proceeded to enlighten them on several facts. I told them that I was a grown man who could do what ever I wanted, and that they could never understand why I had chosen to do what I did. Most of all I said that I wasn't going to put up with their nonsense. Talk about looking a gift horse in the mouth; I was kicking one in the mouth.

Over time, after we were married, there would be more attempts for my parents and us, myself in particular, to reconcile. By this time there was one major sticking point; to accept me, they had to accept her. That was true for both sides of our family. For her family to accept her, they had to accept me. We were furious when it came to that matter. Late one weeknight evening there was a message for me to call my dad. He said that they had accepted what had happened and where we were. He asked that I please give him a call as soon as I got the message.

I returned the call and we were invited to meet them the following Saturday in Selma at Shoney's restaurant at 4 p.m. That was significant to all parties for a couple of reasons. One, it was an attempt to move toward my terms. Second, at that time of the day the place would just about be empty so no one was likely to see either of us. Before this, my parents had made it clear that they would never accept her. They had said she would never be in their house or in their company.

With a nervous stomach and sweaty palms we drove to Selma. When we turned into the parking lot of the restaurant, my parents were already there. There was a great deal of awkwardness as we got out of the car and moved into the restaurant. We all ordered from the menu, but I am not sure that any of us ate. The air was thick with tension and suspicion. What are we really here for? What are boundaries over which we can talk? Time seem to stand still as we sat there. How long can we talk? True enough, we soon ran out of things to comfortably talk about and it was time to go. I had won. I had made them do something they did not want to do. I didn't care how they felt about this incredible situation. It was more proof of a hardened heart.

Chastening 101

4

It seemed as though the bell rang and God said "School is now in session." God's ways are certainly not our ways. Who would have ever connected the sight of the eyes, the smell of the nose, and the hearing of the ears into one incredible strand of strength called conscience? Which one of us would have chosen to use the vividness of the conscience as a tool in the art of correction? God loves us so much that He gave His only Son. He also loves us enough to chase and chasten those who pursue the prodigal life. There is a difference between chastening and judgment. Judgment has to do with condemnation while chastening has to do with correction. Judgment implies finality while chastening implies being allowed to continue the journey. Judgment reveals the absence of relationship, while chastening is proof of belonging, the signature of adoption. "...because the Lord disciplines those he loves..."[7]

My prodigal experience began before October 1993. It was just publicly revealed in October 1993. Approximately two months after remarriage the door opened to the school of chastening. For sure there had been many attempts to get my attention but now it was as though there would be no rest in heaven until the prodigal responded. I admit I had paid very little attention to the concept and for sure it had always applied to others and not me. Now it was as if God said that for years you have run through the road blocks and you have chosen to swim in dirty water. Now you are going to see just how dirty.

What followed was having every area of my life touched except my health. God never chose to take physical health away, as though that was hedged. Every other area was fair game including my work, finances, and relationships, not to mention the other things on the list. Work was pay check driven not having any other purpose or satisfaction. It lacked any greater purpose and was laden with frustration. Frequently it seemed as though you were running in sand. Every other part of life seemed to mirror the same characteristics. All of it was designed to get my attention and to keep it. Getting my attention was the hard part, Keeping it was no problem.

General Norman Swartzkoff was giving a briefing during "Desert Storm". He was asked why so many Iraqis had surrendered. They had been pounded by B-52 bombers. General.Swartzkoff responded that "once a B-52 has flown over your position and dropped its bombs, the second time you hear a B-52 coming your feet just will not let you stay there!"

In the Old Testament, when Eli the priest discovers that his two sons has been having sex with the women who came to the temple, he said" if a man sins against another man, God may mediate for him; but if a man sins against the Lord, who will intercede for him?"[8] That sounds to me like a fatherly way of saying "boys you are on your own." How right he was. When God has you in the woodshed,

46

there is literally nothing any human being can do to help you. There was hope, but, for the time being, no help.

The focus of all of heaven seems to have been riveted on taking care of the business at hand. Correction would be full and complete. In hind sight, it was like heaven was saying "you don't realize what you are, what you have done, and you also don't realize what you are about to experience." In retrospect, the sharpness of the chastening was so clear. It had a beginning, a process, and an ending. Through the prodigal experience, I created a list of enemies. I can't think of a one that I could wish this experience of chastening upon. The effects I might wish, but never the experience. It was too horrific! God was serious and he meant business. This is not an attempt to paint a negative picture of God. God had made a great investment in a wayward child and his love is so deep that it knows no boundaries to retrieve his treasure. While the experience was difficult, God even gave the prodigal the grace to endure it. What great love, to pursue and correct a child in order to bring change. All the while he provided sustaining grace!

Jesus told Peter"… Satan has asked that he may sift you as wheat…"[9] Peter had told Jesus that he would never deny Him. Peter thought denying Christ was unthinkable. If a warm fire, a small damsel, and a pestering question brought out such a vile and violent denial on the part of Peter, what would he have done with real pressure? He didn't have a clue of what it could have been. I liken that to chastening. If with intent God allows some hedges to be dropped and a little bit of hell to intrude, what would it be like if he just totally gave in to the desires of Satan?

Satan can't think of a scar he doesn't like. In my opinion few things bring him laughter like gazing on the scars he has inflicted on people. Imagine his excitement as he observes someone wearing an ugly scar from their choices. Whether it is emotional scars or physical scars, all bring him delight. He loves scars and he loves to scar. He will scar you mentally, physically, emotionally, spiritually, financially, and relationally. He will scar your mind, your body, your soul and your will. The only thing that may bring him more delight that scarring, is watching you wear them. The scars are repulsive to those who see them and often cause such a high level of discomfort among those viewing them that they walk away. Even with the scars, Satan seeks devastation. God seeks restoration.

CRACKS IN THE SHED

Inside the old shed that belonged to my "Papa," you could look through the cracks and see others on the outside. They couldn't see you on the inside. They might have known you were in there, but they couldn't know exactly were you were. From the inside you could see their every move. Much like chastening, many on the outside knew you were in the "shed", but they couldn't see all of that. It was a full blown case of chastening, where God used ruined relationships, financial fiasco, lost credibility and spiritual blight. In each scenario there was pressure and pain. All had a purpose.

In relationships, the very people you sought to get away from now were wanted and needed, but it was too late. My family had been driven away and responded by informing me to stay away from them. People who once viewed you with a level of respect were now suspicious and cold, holding you at bay. Many wanted nothing to do with you at all. The seeds of disrespect and rejection previously planted had now come to full bloom.

Some say that a person has very few "true" friends. I'm not sure how many a "few" is but I will tell you that when you malign and mistreat them there will be even fewer. It was common that in the prodigal experience I treated them with rudeness and with arrogance. I do not begrudge them. Many of them were deeply hurt and confused. Others just didn't know what to do. To a person they would not have had to deal with the situation had I not put them on the spot. Having done so, I was now in the position of needing friends only to I find I had burned way too many bridges. I sat in the cold dampness of isolation. I created it! There was no one to pal around with, go to a game with, or just talk and kid around with. I was in God's chastening shed. There was the deafening sound of silence.

I never had a bill I couldn't pay. While certainly not rich, where my next meal would come from was never a question. That is, until I was in the "shed". In arrogance I thought you could take God given abilities and use them in a secular world for secular purposes and be just fine. So when I decided to give up my God given assignment, I was of the strong opinion that I would make it big time. My first job was a commission only job calling on merchants. The first three days I made a thousand dollars in commissions. I was never fully paid the thousand dollars. The next three months I didn't earn a thousand dollars total. That hardship would continue for an extended period of time. There was the drain of working long hours and driving a lot of miles only to receive commission checks that would amount to four dollars or eleven dollars. Sure there were larger checks, but they were few and far between.

Something is going on here, but I can fix it. Need money? Just borrow it or get a new job. I did both. It was selling door to door with a small salary plus commission. That will take care of the problem. Seems the small salary would end in twelve weeks but by then I would have so much in commission I wouldn't need it! Do you know how short twelve weeks is? Need money? Borrow it. Get a credit card and take a cash advance. Problem solved.

People really don't like to open their door to a stranger or talk about something they think they don't need. Especially when they just got home, supper is getting cold and they have some place to go. What does this mean? No sales, no commission, no check, and no money. Borrow more, get a new credit card, and get a new job. One profession for sixteen years, and in ten months I'm starting my third job. In case you have not noticed, there is a serious case of aimless wandering that has set in.

The third job seemed to have more promise. It was not in sales, I just made appointments so others could sell. The difficulty was that in the end I would be paid on their ability to make a sale. No sales, no check, no money, and borrow more. What do you mean I can't borrow more? With credit lines exhausted and no way to pay the bills, the phone began to ring with a growing list of people who wanted their money.

¤¤¤¤¤¤¤¤

In case you have not noticed, there is a serious case of
aimless wandering that has set in.

¤¤¤¤¤¤¤¤

Making Arrangements

Everybody was affected. There was a family that needed money, collectors that needed paying, and bills on top of bills. It seemed like a sea of people and they all needed money.

You can become skilled in the art of making arrangements, but the problem lies in not having the money to keep those arrangements. There is only so much in the way of personal items that you can sell or pawn. I sold several personal items that included golf equipment some of which I had from my teen years. I attempted to sell my entire library worth several thousand dollars but couldn't find any interested parties. I came within hours of having

50

my only means of transportation repossessed. It was difficult when you could not explain to your children why you could not buy them a soft drink. It hurt because you couldn't explain it. It hurt more that you couldn't do it.

Few of my family or friends ever knew how destitute I had become. Food was scarce, yet God always provided enough. There were more than several weeks where two adults would survive on five dollars worth of groceries. We were in no position to handle any financial surprises.

Once, the transmission in the car began acting up. My children and I were in traffic and it wouldn't go into third gear. The pressure and frustration were such that in anger I looked toward heaven and screamed "What more do you want?" My oldest son looked at me and said "God will help you if you will only ask." Talk about out of the mouth of babes... A friend from the church we were attending helped fix the transmission as a favor. Soon after, the air conditioner in the car went out. For two summers we did without simply because there were no funds available to fix it. I never chose to file bankruptcy, but there was no question I was bankrupt!

There are few pressures in life that compare to financial pressure. The ringing of the phone became a nightmare. In fact the mere ringing of the phone could send terror through my body. "Mr. Walley, we have not received your last payment. Mr. Walley, your account is past due. Mr. Walley we must have a payment tonight in order to keep your account from going to collections." Ring. . . Ring. . . Ring. . . Don't answer the phone any more. The mail became just as bad. "Dear Mr. Walley, we have not received your last payment... Dear Sir, your account has been turned over for collection to our firm...." I answered the phone once after having gotten the mail and the same creditor who had sent me a letter was now calling me and I recall standing in the bedroom with the phone in my hand as the creditor made it very clear what they planned to do to me. As I stood there, a grown man, I found myself crying profusely into the phone for mercy from a person I did not even know.

One morning I had come by the apartment and the phone rang. Sheepishly I answered. The voice on the other end informed me that a truck was on the way to repossess my car. It was the only transportation I had. I needed to make two payments that day before 2:30 and a third by the end of the week. Where would I find that kind of money so quickly? It was simple. Beg, borrow, pawn or sell. I did all four!

More and more I begin to notice that fewer and fewer people had any confidence in anything I said. My children didn't believe me. The few family members I spoke with didn't believe me. Creditors didn't believe me. There is no way to evaluate the loss of credibility. It was nearly impossible to regain credibility. With some people there is absolutely no human way to regain it. When every thing you say begins to be questioned, you are left in a world of disbelief for which there are few remedies.

A New Place and a New Life

When I came to Montgomery the high blue autumn sky watched as I moved about city in search of a place to live. I secured a local apartment guide and went from apartment complex to complex in search of the perfect place to start over. Once I reached the decision and paid the deposit I set about to find furniture. Visits were made to two home furnishing stores and items were picked out as though I had no cares in the world and money was no object.

The deals were so good that with my good credit I would not have to face paying for the purchases until many months later. Like a balloon in the wind I was carried along by the surge of disobedience. I had not a care in the world and was oblivious to the obvious. It doesn't take a rocket scientist to see the clouds were gathering and the shift in the moral compass indicts trouble was ahead. But it would not be today. Not now. And besides, I was sure it would not be anything I couldn't handle.

The apartment was a nice first floor two bedroom unit with a screened porch. It had a little over nine hundred square feet and a swimming pool. The rent was reasonable and this was going to be a great place to "start over." With new furniture that included a TV, sleeper sofa, recliner, dining table, kitchen table, and a bedroom suite I was good to go. There were a set of steps that you came down after entering the foyer of the building. Over the two year period, what started out as a place to start over would become a hell hole.

During the chastening period, when the waves of chastening were at their highest, the apartment would be a place that was an emotional prison. With all the effects of my choices now threaded together to bring about maximum results, the starting over place became a place of dread. The thought of going to the apartment created anxiety. Being in a position where much of my time would be spent in the apartment, I found myself going to extremes to keep from being there. The space within the apartment had seemingly shrunk. The sound of the door opening and closing was a sound of dread. The smell of the place was certainly pleasant, but it too became more unbearable. Furniture that was at one point a symbol of independence and determination was now a burden to pay for. Couple these things along with the sound of the mail man in the foyer opening the mail box and the dread would become saturating.

Other than my children, who came every other weekend we very rarely had others in the apartment. The absence of family and friends only magnified the real emptiness and loneliness the place had now come to represent. Regardless of how much you think you love someone, if you are not right with the Lord there will be difficult times. If you don't put him first, if you don't surrender yourself completely to him, if you don't seek him out then there are few words that can define the troubles that are ahead. They are brought about by the situation you are in. At least, that is what I found from our experience. We felt that we had such a deep and growing love for each other, and yet the situation had become so intense and stressful.

Guilt and Pressure

There were several factors that were adding to the intensity and stress. Guilt nagged and nagged the two of us. Two mates had been hurt. Children had been devastated. Two homes had been ruined. A church had been embarrassed. Some may have believed that we didn't have the ability to feel any guilt. We would often blame each other for the situation we found ourselves in. When we would talk to our families we would be careful that the other one was not in the room because we felt such guilt. Many times each of us would break down in tears from the guilt we carried. More than once I found her sitting in the middle of the bed sobbing with guilt. I had my own places to go and cry and I found myself there with growing frequency.

One evening, after talking to the boys, I went into the second bedroom. In that room was a set of bunk beds that I had gotten from my sister. They had actually been my brothers and mine when we were children. The closet in that room contained my personal library. I returned after dark one evening and threw all my office stuff into the car in a hurried way before someone saw me. Now everything from my office was crammed into the closet. As I came into the room, I opened the closet door looking for something that was actually in the opposite end of the closet. There in front of me was my calling in the form of my study library. Like a cold tire iron to the face, I quickly turned away only to be faced with the bunk beds. Before I knew it I was prostrate on the floor, crying like a child. I was consumed by my guilt. I remained in that position for quite some time, unable to get up and move.

Often I would go out side and walk through the apartment complex when the sting of guilt would show up. When guilt was at its worst, I would start in on her for the situation we were in. The pressure grew!

Money also served to create enormous pressure between the two of us. When we would look at how little money we had to buy groceries, the pressure and tension would start. We had both come from relatively secure homes. To find ourselves in a situation of not being able to have enough food was unbelievable. We found ourselves carefully planning our meals and what each meal would consist of. We never added one thing when we went to the store and those meals were revisited weekly because we knew how much it would cost. This was not how life is supposed to be!

What were we going to pay? What were we not going to pay? How could two intelligent people wind up in such financial hardship? Most of all, we didn't want anyone in our family to know that we were really destitute. When the phone would ring in the evening, it prompted the question "is it a bill collector for you or for me?" How much of this could you take? How long could it go on?

Without question one of the most stressful and irritating things was trying to blend our families into one. They were all shocked and mad. They did not care one thing about being "blended." The first Christmas Day I spent alone in the apartment. I was to pick up my children on Christmas night and she could be with her children the entire day. It was the longest Christmas day I had spent since my grandfather died on Christmas Day of 1974. I vowed I would never allow one of us to be alone on the holidays for the convenience of family, who really didn't want to accept that we were together. When they refused to accept our desire, it infuriated both of us. We would draw our lines in the sand. We would then digress into an argument over how much pressure each was applying to his or her family to make them accept our situation. It became expected that if a family member who didn't want to treat us with respect would show up where we were, he or she could leave or we would leave. Numerous times those scenes were played out in an ugly fashion. Blending a family is hard work in the best of scenarios. It is nearly impossible when you are trying to force people to do something against their wills.

¤¤¤¤¤¤¤¤

They were all shocked and mad. They did not care one thing about being "blended"

¤¤¤¤¤¤¤¤

Dry Soul

The picture of the wind blowing the dry sand of the western desert with its dry riverbeds and blowing tumble weeds becomes a good description of a soul with a serious leak. You can get what you want and while doing so get leanness in your soul. It happened to the Israelites and it can to you. It happened to me.

Psalms 106:15 says of God toward his people "…so he gave them what they asked for, but sent a wasting disease upon them."[10] It describes God letting the people have what they wanted but He sent leanness to their soul. A lean soul is a spectacle of mistreatment. It is the picture of a soul that aches from starvation and maltreatment. It is also the reflection of a soul that has lost power, perspective and its priorities. Fellowship was glaringly absent. It functions from memory. Intimacy with God is not designed to be

56

from memory, but alive and fresh each day. I could sit in the pew, but the soul was parched. I could sing the songs but the soul still ached.

Extended periods of time away from personal prayer and bible study become the norm. Church was a take it or leave it proposition. My lifestyle became a large picture of compromise. I wanted to reach the place where my conscience didn't disturb me and finally it happened. The Holy Spirit had been told to be quiet time and again and he has been grieved and quenched. Life is now lived as though there is not a God at all. Decisions were based on what felt good or seemed right to me. There was no longer a moral compass or a need for one. It was a full time job convincing my self that this really is what I wanted and everything was alright. There was no time for serious questions or soul searching. Spiritual things meant absolutely nothing to you.

The dry soul was one starved for food and attention. I never stopped attending Church. I went Sunday morning and night. During the prodigal period I lived with a woman ten months without being married. It seemed right but I knew it was wrong. All of the other things we had done, like lying, cheating on our mates, and abandoning our witness, had numbed our consciences. I had long since given up a personal time with the Lord. I no longer maintained or guarded a time of Bible study and prayer. Giving up that time came quite easy by allowing it to become a time without meaning. Less and less time and focus were given until it was gone. Church was just the "respectable" thing to do. Fortunately, it did serve to keep me in proximity to the tug of God.

Parents Perspective

We were beaten down by worry, disappointment, and despair. Never before had we been driven to our knees and to His word like this. The first holidays were perhaps the saddest time of all. Thanksgiving had been selected as our family gathering to celebrate both Thanksgiving and share Christmas gifts as we were not able to be together for Christmas. The holidays had just begun to return to a time of celebration after having lost PaPa Jones on Christmas day several years earlier.

With Steve becoming a prodigal in late October, the holiday spirit would be put to the test immediately. He came to the gathering with his two small sons. It was a time of strain and intense anger. How he could do this was the concern of the entire family. Tears and pleading for him to do the right thing were met with hostility and refusal. As we watched him leave with the two confused and helpless children, it felt as though our heart wanted to jump from within our chest.

How long could this go on? How would we ever return to some sense of normality? How could you be expected to take so much? Our eyes were swollen from hours of crying.

Our hearts were broken from such betrayal. Our pride was devastated from such public humiliation. We had been hurt and that hurt was turning more and more to anger. Pages written in our daily journals would be ripped out so no one could see just what our true feelings were. Our personal Christianity was being put to the test. A test we were not sure we could pass!

Consequences, Consequences, Consequences

5

What is a divorce? It is the total destruction of what once were two people's dreams. The dream of spending their lives together, of watching each transition through the various changes that life invariably brings, seeing and sharing in the experiences of childrearing and aging parents. A framed piece of cross stitch said that "in marriage when one cries the other taste the salt." Divorce is the bomb that ultimately impacts every dream a couple can have.

I should be very clear that my ex-wife was in no way responsible for my choices. At the time I certainly blamed her and others, but it was not her fault. No human being should ever have to go through what I put my ex-wife through. The same could be said of my partner's ex-husband. I can speak more to my ex-wife and yet I can't really speak at all. I know what she went through in both a personal and public way. Yet, to the contrary I really don't know what she went through at all. Clearly it was hurtful, but how could I describe that level of pain. I know that she had to deal with the public embarrassment of my choices while taking care of her needs and the needs of the children.

How could I begin to claim that I understand her embarrassment? I know there was confusion, anger, frustration and deep disappointment because she had invested a great deal in the success of our lives. Now a decision that would affect the rest of her life was made by the very man who had committed to spend the rest of his life with her. Over and over I had been very deceptive and untruthful with her. She had been lied to, manipulated, overlooked, and cheated on. Perhaps more than anything she must have been made to feel that she was losing her mind. To her credit she tried in her way to make it work and to find solutions to the questions. She gave every chance for the children to have a safe and steady home environment.

One of the many consequences is in knowing how you hurt another person. Yet, she was not just another person. She was the very one who shared herself with me in every way and who gave birth to my sons. She was the very one who believed in me when others did not, encouraged me when I needed it most, and tolerated me when others would not. Even this description is shallow when describing who she was.

The cold reality of consequences is that your mind is very much aware of what you did to the other person. One can only beg forgiveness and hope that God has a short memory when He gets to you. I remember the attempts to get me to reconcile even after I had publicly embarrassed her by leaving and being with someone else. All those attempts were met with a flagrant refusal. I better understand why God has a special place for the widows and orphans.

Missing Out

My first trip back to the house was under the cover of darkness. I went to leave some money when no one was home. I quickly found the locks were changed. Through the grapevine I heard some people were advising that I might physically hurt the children and even her. That never entered my mind. On one occasion I went back and several weeks had passed since my initial leaving. By this time the children were very confused. They had no doubt overheard some of the concerns expressed by others along with just the impact of the event. The oldest was afraid to go with me. At first he refused to even get in the car. Finally he did, but we never got out of the drive way. It took several trips back just to get him to go with me around the block. The youngest was almost unaware of what was taking place.

Once I picked them up and went to a motel in Mobile. We checked in late in the afternoon and before we could eat supper the oldest was already talking of going home. I became angry and accused everyone of sabotaging the visits which did not help the situation. I ended up taking them back home that evening before ten. When the oldest would cry, the youngest would follow. It was clear that my children were not sure of my love for them and were very uncomfortable with me. With some encouragement from their mother, I began talking with them by phone every day.

The times we shared were at best awkward. There was a couple of hours driving distance between us, so if I picked them up and returned home, it would be a four hour trip to be repeated two days later. Often I would rent a room for the weekend to stay close. That was weird because of the absence of a place to go. Finances would soon take away the options of getting a room. We were left then with the two hour treks for them and four hour treks for me.

✿✿✿✿✿✿✿✿

It was clear that my children were not sure of my love for them and were very uncomfortable with me.

✿✿✿✿✿✿✿✿

All in all the boys were flexible given the enormity of the adjustments they had to make. The oddity was adjusting to the woman they viewed as responsible for hurting their mother and disrupting their lives. They also had to adjust to having an absentee father. The adjustment to a position of financial hardship was something I'm sure they felt. I would talk to them every day but soon their everyday absence in my life would start to take its toll. A phone call is one thing. Being present is another. Talking with them about what they did today in school is not the same as being there to help them with their assignments.

I am not sure exactly what all I missed out on with my boys. I do know there are some things that are obvious. I missed out on their ball playing. I had to schedule to make a game. I seldom if ever made a practice. Coaching or helping with the team was simply out of the question. I also missed out on various school activities. I recall attending maybe two PTA meetings. I would arrange to be at "special" activities such as a field trip, a class play, parent's lunch and so forth. The involvement from a distance is a limited one.

The most important things I missed were the spiritual things in my son's lives. When the oldest was scheduled to be baptized they still attended the church I served as pastor when this prodigal life was made known. The interim pastor told me that I was not to attend the baptism because of what I had done. I did not go and missed the experience. When the youngest made his decision and was scheduled for baptism, I was again informed that I was not to attend. I missed that experience as well. I regret deeply not showing up at either regardless of the feelings of others. What I regret most is not being present to share in the experience of my sons coming to find and know the Savior who loves them most.

Another thing that I missed out on is the growing changes in the lives of my children. When I saw them every two weeks it is amazing how much they have changed, whether it is the physical change in appearance or gestures, or the more subtle changes in their maturity. The truth is they are changing and I not only missed it, I was now behind for not having been a part of it.

Lost Influence

Lost influence is an aspect that is often overlooked. By vacating the day to day responsibilities of fatherhood, one unintended consequence is lost influence in my children's lives. Other people emerged to influence my children and I had no control over who those people were and what their values were. I was not present and may not have known that they had been inserted into the lives of the children until well after the fact. Fortunately, those who have been involved with my children have been good people, but the truth is lost influence was still a fact. They gave of themselves to spend time with the boys, whether it was taking them to the "farm" to work, to ride four wheelers, or to various other activities like "boys day out" where they would go to breakfast with others. The reality of not being there day to day is difficult to deal with.

Decisions were made about their lives and I was not there. I was not consulted and I understand some of that. I had to deal with the sharpness that others who ordinarily would have minimal place with my children were exerting influence and often making decisions in their world. While there was not anyone involved with them that I would not have wanted to be, it is the underlying fact that I have relinquished my role in their life. That is the issue which I have struggled with.

Fresh Start and Fresh Problems

When all the divorces were final, we decided that we would get married. We were already living together and had been all along. We wanted to try and take care of the matter as quickly as possible. We called a number of states to ascertain the waiting time required from the time you got your license until you could marry. South Carolina had a time frame that suited us. We began to make plans to go to Charleston to be married. Arriving in the city, we secured a hotel, and went to the courthouse to get the license. We called and arranged for a minister to perform the ceremony. He had a very nice courtyard where it could be done. We set it up for the following afternoon and arranged for a horse drawn carriage to take us from the hotel to the courtyard. Everything seemed to be in place.

The following afternoon, as I began to dress for the occasion, the nerves began to churn. Perhaps it was the idea of just getting married. I suspect it was more than that. The fact was, one more bridge was about to be burned. There was a silent haunting that it was not right and what had taken place to make it a possibility was not right. The illusion and mind game was that you would have a life others would only dream about. For sure it was a ceremony tainted by conscience. In a matter of minutes the vows were said and the rings were exchanged. Now, everyone would just have to like it. On your marks, ready, set, here we come! We returned to Montgomery, rings on our fingers and confidence in our heart. I was confident and in charge. Little did I realize the consequences were adding up!

Someone has said that your attitude will affect your altitude. My attitude stunk! The more intense chastening became, the more it affected my attitude. Everyone was against me. No one would give me a chance. People didn't care what happened to you. No one is going to offer any help whatsoever. In my view the circumstances I was in were the responsibility of everyone else. Things had not turned out the way I had led myself to believe, but it was not my fault. I felt trapped and controlled. I started believing I had nothing to offer to anyone. I had nothing to offer my new wife, my children, or an employer.

Church did not necessarily offer any relief either. We had been attending a church in Montgomery but we blended in and remained anonymous. Each Sunday the pastor would come out to the congregation before the service started to greet those in attendance. He would always come over and speak but it never became more personal than that. Eventually after service one Sunday, I walked to the door and waited for everyone to leave. With no one around I reintroduced myself and told him a little bit of the information about myself and what had happened. I requested that before any consideration of joining that church was given, that I really would like for him to come by and see us. I wanted to try and be honest with him and give him as much information as he felt was necessary. Weeks went by and he never came to see us. I was unsuccessful at even getting an appointment with him and then we began to notice that on Sundays, he quit coming over to where we were sitting for the routine pre service greeting. It was obvious that we really were not wanted there, so we moved on.

At one point I had sent out over two hundred resumes. I went to look through the jobs available at the State Unemployment Office. It seemed like you were staring into space. I would get all dressed up and go to an interview and nothing would happen. I would drive back over to the state office and get on the computer and search for what was available. Standing at the computer, I would wonder what the people were thinking about me. What was I doing here? How long before something would go right in my life? How long could I stand this? The motivation was waning and the attitude was souring. It was all someone else's fault.

Interstate 65 runs north and south through Alabama. Often I would leave the boys on a Sunday afternoon and head north on the interstate toward Montgomery. The ride up the road would be an exercise of brutality. Between the bouts of paralyzing guilt and incredible anger, there would be moments of clear thinking. The markings of the roadway would fade to a blur mixed in the salt of the tears. There would be flashes of the boy's faces and of the fun we might have shared. What would follow would be the desire to go and be with them. It would feel as though someone had stuck a hot branding iron straight into my heart. I was caught between the tug of the Spirit of God, the innocence of two small boys, and a stubborn will. The stubborn will won out. The one hour and forty five minute drive would be a torture cell in motion. It never got any easier.

The most useful thing a believer can be this side of heaven is a witness for Christ. I had been trained in various methods of presenting my faith. The crux of any faith sharing technique is your validity as a witness. Without it there is nothing to share. When I became involved in the ways of the world, I lost my ability to present a credible witness for Christ. In the front end I didn't care. After the heart softens a bit and I saw the damaged done by my disobedience one of the things I could see most clearly was a lost witness.

On the east coast an Amtrak train and freight collided. In doing the inquiry it was found that the flagman had been beside the track. He was asked if he had been waving his red flag to which he said yes. What he did not realize was that his "red" flag after having been out the elements had faded from "red" to "yellow". It had lost its color! A flag that was to be a display of danger was now only a warning to "proceed with caution." Ephesians 2:10 says that "...we are his workmanship..."[11] We are intended to be a brilliant display of what God can do in any human's heart. Clearly the choices I had made allowed the flag of my salvation to lose its color. There was no distinction between my life and someone who had never personally accepted Christ into their life.

Parents Perspective

As we walked into the broken home the first Christmas to see a Christmas tree with a few presents underneath, a wave of grief and sadness came over us unlike anything we had ever experienced. While we have both lost our parents to death this was different. The dead were still living! What consequences would he have to suffer? What consequences would those caught in the crossfire of his behavior have to suffer? Only time could reveal. One thing for sure, it would be no small matter.

There was absolutely nothing as parents we could do to intervene in the consequences. We tried. There are just some things you can do nothing about. You wanted things to be right and lessons to be learned, but the consequences were in the hand of the Lord. In her book "Prodigals and those that Love Them," Ruth Bell Graham reflected on her handling of their son Franklin being a prodigal. She told of being awakened in the night and it was the voice of the Lord saying to her; "Stop studying the problem and start studying the promises".[1] This became our prayer indeed "… that in all things God works for the good of those who love him…" [2] For sure we could not see any way for something positive and productive to come from this. Never had we known such pain, disappointment, and humiliation from any of our family. This was tough and it was deep. It did not seem to be going away.

Grace and Forgiveness

6

Brokenness is the one and only ingredient that God recognizes and uses to bring one back to Him. Brokenness is the point where you become willing to do whatever it takes, coming to the place where even if you are not willing, you are willing to be made willing. There is nothing or no one that you are willing to hold onto. It becomes essential that whatever it takes, you are willing to do. Brokenness is the point when you are literally sick of your sin. But it is more than that.

It involves not only being sick of the circumstances and consequences of your sin, but more importantly it is being sick over the cause of your sin. It is right that you should grieve over where you have wound up. It is even more right that you should grieve over what is in you that brings you to that point. It is coming to face reality squarely in the face and admit that what you do is a mirror of what you are. The impact of the sight of one's self at that point is both spiritually and physically nauseating. It drives you to see what you have been unwilling to see before. You taste what you have been unwillingly to taste before. You see what you have been not only relative to this prodigal experience but you also see roots from the past that have contributed to the present. How many times have you really been a prodigal at heart long before now?

You accept about yourself what you never wanted to believe before. Brokenness is brutally truthful and incredibly clear. It leaves no room to wonder or doubt. The issue is you, and what is on the inside of you. It is about your personal responsibility for the choices that you have made and the ingredients within you that allowed those particular choices to be made. In my opinion, anything short of being sick of the causes of sin only leaves one to lament the consequences of sin and never to deal with the real issue.

Upon being broken over the cause of sin there is the weight of guilt that can only be relieved and released by the finished work of Christ on the cross. It is openly agreeing with Him that everything you have experienced consequentially is because of what you have allowed to grow inside of you and that now you have reached a point where you must find His forgiveness in the matter. Brokenness is the awareness that if He doesn't forgive you then there is no forgiveness. There is no moving on. It is coming to a point of such utter helplessness and the burden is so great that it feels as though you cannot breathe.

✿✿✿✿✿✿✿✿

Brokenness is the one and only ingredient God uses to
bring one back to Himself.

✿✿✿✿✿✿✿✿

If there is no forgiveness, then there is no need to breathe. You are broken and must be fixed. He alone is the one who understands the intricate workings of the human makeup and the soul for which He died. He alone is the Master whose touch can offer the assurance of forgiveness and sort through the mangled mess of disobedience. In my experience there must be the mixing of your sin and His grace. Forgiveness is immediate! Restoration is a process! Both must begin with brokenness.

I well remember reaching that point of brokenness. I can remember the moment when I knew that I had gone as far I could go and what was wrong was inside of me. I remember the horror of facing my sin. It came in what I consider to be the deeply personal and private revelations of sin after sin after sin that the Spirit of God brought to the theater of my mind. I remember the sweet brush of forgiveness across my heart as He whispered "forgiven" with each confession to Him that each was true. Consequences were not changed, but the cause was exposed and addressed. You are naïve should you think that confession and forgiveness mean the removal of consequences. It could mean that, but it really means the cause has been addressed.

Broken Pots and Mended Clay

Upon reaching a point of brokenness, God began to restore. True enough there were some things that were not going to be put back. Some bridges had been burned in the time lived in my stubborn response to God. But God is able to take a broken pot and shape it into mended clay. God began to do a variety of things one of which was restoring some old friendships. Early in my journey a friend had gotten my number from my parents and called and left a message. "Steve, I'm hearing some things and I don't know if they are true or not. I don't like what I'm hearing but if you need to talk please give me a call." It took almost twenty months for me to call and when I did he offered me grace and friendship. My parents and I had been estranged for almost three years. That relationship was restored without interruption at the point of brokenness

In November of 1996 I was asked to fill in for a Sunday at a church in Selma, Alabama. The turmoil of feeling I should and the turmoil of feeling I shouldn't were unreal. Reluctantly I agreed but felt it necessary to tell the pastor of my past before filling in. He offered me grace with substance by giving me opportunity. The contrast between belonging and not belonging persisted throughout the entire Sunday's responsibilities.

Shortly afterward the church in Montgomery where we had been attending asked me to supply. This pastor was a guy whom I credit with saving my life. At a point when one pastor refused to talk with me I had felt I had no place to turn. Later on I went through the same routine with this pastor with a completely different result. He not only came but he brought with him grace and truth. He offered a great deal of encouragement but was brutally honest. He offered two ears and a pair of shoulders that night and many other days and nights that followed. When he spoke I had learned to listen but with the invitation to supply for him came the feelings of, "should I or shouldn't I." The pastor assured me it would be a good experience for the church and me. The church had over a thousand in attendance in the three morning worship services. The reception and warmth extended to me was encouraging. I inquired beforehand if the pastor was sure my filling the pulpit would not create problems for him. He responded that he had been serving as their pastor for over ten years and if they were going to be unforgiving, he wanted to find out now. They were very forgiving. The pastor encouraged me to become willing to let God lead and use me however He saw fit.

The Dawning of a New Day

As God began the process of restoration things started coming together. Restoration is a process. Forgiveness is instant but restoration takes time. But the process was underway and it began to be evidenced in several ways. One was the opportunity to fill in. Another was that the financial picture and job scenario began to change. With the chastening period in full swing, money was always in demand. During chastening when the money came it went nowhere. But when God began to restore, financial needs were met in the most incredible way.

The Christmas of 1996 was looking as one disaster waiting to happen. We had absolutely no money to buy any presents. None! Not one red cent! We were in serious trouble with creditors. We made a list and priced what we would buy if we had the money. It was insurmountable. One week before Christmas a friend from church came by to visit. Upon leaving he shook my hand and instructed me to take what was in his hand. Inside an envelope was a rolled up stack of money. When it was counted it totaled the amount that was needed to buy Christmas, including the taxes, with a few dollars left over! These were among the first clear outward signals that God had embraced the broken and contrite heart and the restoration process was beginning.

A couple of weeks before Christmas I was offered a job by a long lost family friend I had not seen in twenty years. He had heard of my situation and called to talk. In the course of our conversation he discussed an opening he had in a business of which he was part owner. I made the trip to Mobile to take a look at the opportunity and both sides liked what they saw. I was given the job and the start date was set for first week of January 1997. The new job seemed to be a golden opportunity as I would be working with a psychiatrist conducting groups for his clients. It also posed some immediate obstacles. One was relocating to Mobile and finding a place to rent given my current credit problems. Another was handling the transportation issue. We only had one car and my wife would have to stay in Montgomery for three months or until the apartment rented. And then there was the money issue. How would we make it the first few weeks until some money came in?

I had to be in Mobile for work on Monday at 8a.m. The Sunday prior we had attended church and came back to the apartment to face the reality of where we were. I had a job and did not have the transportation or money to get there. We debated our options and could not find any solutions. About three in the afternoon we started to pray. Within the hour a friend called to see how things were going. I sensed that God had initiated the call so I felt very comfortable sharing the dilemma I was in. He quickly arranged and paid for the rental of a car for one week to help me get to Mobile. One problem solved. A family member called shortly afterward and when he learned of the situation he made a few calls and in short order I had a sofa to sleep on for a few nights. We counted the cash and we had five dollars. I took two and left her with three. The rental car had a full tank and I was good to go. I came to Mobile in a rented car, slept on a borrowed sofa, and had two dollars in my pocket!

The first day on the job my new employer informed me that we were going to "lunch". "Lunch" it turns out was a luncheon with the Honorable Richard Shelby, United States Senator from Alabama. I don't remember what the conversations were about, but I do remember sitting there and sensing the impression of the Lord that, "I love you." He did not make me any promises, just "I love you and as you are welcomed in to the presence of this one who you think is so powerful by my grace and forgiveness you are welcomed into my presence." I also remember wondering if those in the room knew that I had gotten there in a rental car, had slept on a borrowed sofa, and had two dollars to my name? While I wished they knew that I didn't have but the two dollars to my name, I was also glad they did not know that my life had reached such a point.

During the middle of the week my employer and I talked and the conversation got around to my current situation. Somehow, I had managed to get by on the two bucks that I had. As I discussed my transportation issues he informed me he had an extra vehicle I could use for a short while. He said it was available when I needed it. At the end of the week he walked into my office with a white envelope and told me someone had come by the front desk and left it for him with my name on it. I opened it and there were several one hundred dollar bills inside. I stood in silence, fully aware God was providing for me and He was bringing about a new day in my life.

I returned the rental car at the end of the week and the friend who had rented it told me he had made a reservation for me at a hotel in Mobile for the next week. The borrowed sofa was still available, but this would give me and them more privacy. I could not help but stand in amazement at all God had done to confirm His forgiveness was real and I needed to move on.

✿✿✿✿✿✿✿

I stood in silence, fully aware God was providing for me
and He was bringing about a new day in my life.

✿✿✿✿✿✿✿

In the second week I made contact with a old friend from my teenage years. He came over to the hotel and we talked for hours. He is in the wall covering business and offered for me to help him when I got off in the evening. It proved to be a good opportunity to earn some additional money and was it ever needed. During the week I called another old friend from school days in Mobile. As we talked, he told me he had recently gone through a divorce and that he had an extra room in his apartment. I was welcome to come and spend as much time as I needed to get my feet on the ground. It became overwhelming what God was doing to provide.

The following weekend I returned to Montgomery. A man who had become a friend of mine came over and asked how things were going. I recounted the things that God had done to show overwhelming grace and forgiveness. He asked how long we had before the lease was up on our apartment. I told him we had three months left and that some people had looked at it but they were not able to get it. He told me he would buy up the lease as soon as I found a place in Mobile. Man, God was clearly at work!

I came back to Mobile and started looking for a place. I had a great concern over credit checks being run because I really didn't know what would show up. On the weekends we would look for a place, but nothing seemed to be working out. One Tuesday evening I saw an ad in the paper for a townhouse near where I worked. I called and the voice on the other end described a place that sounded like what I was looking for and she sounded desperate to have someone take over the lease. She needed to move out of state to be with her ill mother. I hopped in the car and drove over to take a look. I hoped that this would be the place. She told me that the building was privately owned and she had been there for three years. She and the land lord were on great terms and she had been told by him to find someone with whom she was comfortable and he would let him take over the lease. I told her I was sure I wanted it, but we would need to look at it on Friday. When we both saw the place, we were sure. The landlord came by and I signed the lease and he never asked me any questions regarding my credit.

On Sunday I informed my friend at church that we had gotten a place and he bought out the lease in Montgomery. He owned a furniture store and when it was time for us to move, he told me he was going to send his employees over to move us at no expense to us!

After we got moved and unpacked she began to look for a job. Within a few weeks the opportunity opened up for her to work with a local bank. She had been working for a bank while we were in Montgomery. We both had work that paid, something we had not had for many months.

New Opportunities, New Questions and New Grace

One evening I remember answering the phone, guessing it was probably a family member. The caller on the other end identified herself as being on the search committee from Myrtlewood Baptist Church in Myrtlewood, Alabama. The question was, "would you fill in for us this Sunday?" My brain went dead. Where is this coming from? Is this a joke? The last thing you want to do is get back up in front of people feeling like the rotten banana peel that hasn't quite made it to the garbage can. "Sure I would be glad to. Tell me how to find your church?" It just seems to have come out before I knew what I was saying. Have you lost your mind? I called her back to squirm out of this commitment. "You don't know what you are asking; I don't think you understand where I've been and what I've done. I'm divorced!" Those words seemed so strange coming from my lips; my life. Me divorced!

This was supposed to be enough ammunition to scare away any potential 'fill in' assignment. "We know all about your experience; we just want you to fill in this Sunday." I agreed to supply the following Sunday. I was then asked to do so two weeks later. On that occasion I was asked if I would consider being available for the next several weeks. I was very uncomfortable with where this seemed to be going, but I knew that I had nothing to do with my being there and I didn't want to do anything disobedient to the Lord.

In mid July the search committee asked me if I would consider taking the church on a regular basis. The size of the church would dictate that it would be a weekend assignment. The church had a home that I could stay in on the weekend. It was however, one hundred forty five miles one way from my home.

Reasoning started in. I didn't want to expose myself to exploration of my past. How would I reconcile the theological questions of divorce and leading in worship? How would I deal with the awkwardness of a blended family? How do I deal with feelings of not belonging and being out of the loop for almost four years? The questions were in my opinion legitimate and haunting. The shame cloud was working overtime in particular. You're a second class citizen. You don't deserve to be in that role. You are a spectacle to the ministry. You have had your chance. People will not respect you when they hear what you have done. Exactly where is the hole that I can crawl into and cover myself over.

I thought it best to suggest that I would make myself available while they continued to look for the right person. They in turn were convinced that I should be open to taking on the assignment. I agreed to give it more prayer and thought. From the time in prayer and reflection it became clear to me that God was making an impression on me; I had had nothing to do with opening this door and the last time I took it upon myself to simply take my life into my hands and do as I pleased, the consequences had been severe. I came to the conclusion this was very serious and I should not dismiss it. I found myself in a serious dilemma.

The end result would be that I would have to deal with the haunting questions and let the committee move forward. If the door closed, I then would be relieved to know that I was not the one to close it.

The committee asked to meet with me and we started talking. I wanted to be sure that nothing was kept back and that all areas were addressed. We talked about the prodigal experience and answered all the questions. While I don't remember all the questions of that afternoon, I do remember thinking to my self, why am I putting myself through this? Though I answered their questions honestly, it was still incredibly fresh and painful. I decided to not go any further. It was just too much to have to deal with.

I wasn't sure what they would do as a church or how many times I would have to answer the questions. Would I be willing to go into a question and answer time before the entire congregation? Why should I have to subject myself to any further and continued humiliation? So the game plan was to just let them move on and I would move on quietly.

¤¤¤¤¤¤¤¤

I do remember thinking to myself why am I putting myself through this?

¤¤¤¤¤¤¤¤

Just when I had resolved it in my mind, the committee told me that they were comfortable with where I was now and that they wanted to go further. The dilemma surfaced again about my knowingly taking my life into my own hands. I knew that I did not want to return to the shed for any reason. The sights, sounds, and sensations of that experience were so clear that a second trip was not wanted. It became clear to me that I had to be willing to answer any questions and walk through any door in order to be obedient to Him. I did not then and nor do I now have answers to all the theological questions that people might have about having such an experience in one's past. I told the committee that as far as I was concerned, I would walk through the door as long as they wanted to move forward. They wanted to move forward and did so. They presented their recommendation to the church, along with the history. The church voted unanimously to call me and I said I would accept. What a great place to go and find grace and restoration!

On my first trip to Myrtlewood the engine in my car burned up. I had to find alternate transportation in order to even get to the church. The mechanic informed me the engine would have to be completely rebuilt. The exact cost could not be determined. His best guess was around fifteen hundred to two thousand dollars. The only thing I knew to do was tell him to fix it and I would figure out how to pay for it. I still owed on the car and could not in my mind see paying for a car that was not running.

When the car was repaired he called. I could come and get it. I arrived at the repair shop and anxious to find out how much the repair bill was and then figure out how to pay it. He told me it was over seventeen hundred dollars and then informed me that it had been taken care of. The party did not wish for me to know who they were. I was completely numb. God had once again in such a short period of time met my needs. It was further evidence of His attempt to restore. Later I was able to find the party involved and tell them what evidence of grace they offered through their gift.

In a matter of a few months the opportunity came to start working with men who had charges for domestic violence. I shared responsibilities for developing a program that the courts in five south Alabama counties could use as a referral source. My prodigal experience had begun in Escambia County Alabama in a town called Atmore. Among the first places I was assigned in domestic violence work was, Atmore, working with a Judge who had previously served as my ex-wife's attorney. God has such a sense of humor.

God was gracious enough to bless my work in the area of domestic violence. In the fall of 1997 my friend and I started an agency in Mobile that would provide a resource for the court for domestic violence cases. In 1999 I moved over to Baldwin County, which is across the bay from Mobile, to start my own agency to handle the court cases for domestic violence. God has been so good.

Parents Perspective

The more we searched the scriptures and prayed, the more God's grace worked. Then came the day when we knew beyond any doubt we could accept this prodigal as he was. He belongs to God. In accepting the prodigal, it does not mean we accept the sin. It means we look beyond his faults and see his need just as the Heavenly father has done for us.

God is in the business of redeeming and restoring. He is not willing that any should perish and that includes that one who has defied the Lord God in every way. Patiently and tenderly God began to mend the brokenness and take away our bitterness and unforgiving spirit. How great is the feeling when healing begins and then there is such a release when it is complete. How wonderful the grace He provides for such an ordeal.

Thank you, Lord, for giving us the strength to live through the difficult times. We stand as a testament to the faithfulness of God even when you think it is unfair and painful. He is faithful!

From here to wherever

7

Young John Mark stood at the center of a heated debate. His personal failure resulted in tension and conflict between Paul and his companion Barnabas. Paul wanted nothing else to do with the young failure. Barnabas wanted to extend grace and include Mark in the ministry of the two men. Acts tells us that the disagreement was so strong between the two that they parted company with Paul taking Silas and Barnabas taking his young cousin Mark. It reads like this "They had such a sharp disagreement that they parted company. Barnabas took Mark and sailed for Cyprus, but Paul chose Silas and left..."[12].

There are at least two scenarios to ponder. One is that of Mark. He had abandoned the ministry in which Paul and Barnabas had shared. There is wide speculation as to Mark's going home. Among the speculation was a potential dislike for Paul's approach and leadership. Others have speculated that Mark might have been ill. Mark may very well have been homesick! Whatever is the background Mark was aware that he has left the ministry. He knew the echo's of his own conscience. He remembers the looks on their faces as they were told he was leaving. He recalls the sting of wondering if he was making the right decision. No one has to tell him about his failure. If you were in Mark's shoes with a choice of who to go with, would you chose to go with one who tended toward legalistic harshness or with one who offered compassion? Would you sign on with one who you felt wanted to remind you of your failure or with one who understood that he too was flesh and blood?

A second scenario was that of Barnabas. Why would he want to include the young man who already had a track record of failure? They were cousins and blood is thicker than water. Perhaps he felt a responsibility to the young follower. Could it be there was a stark contrast in the way Paul and Barnabas viewed John Mark? When Paul saw Mark, he saw failure; when Barnabas saw Mark, he saw forgiveness. Paul saw a problem and Barnabas saw potential. Paul viewed Mark as a distraction but Barnabas viewed Mark as a disciple. Barnabas chose Mark and I guarantee you Mark chose Barnabas.

Barnabas then led Mark back through the same area where he had previously failed, helping him to face his failure and move forward in a productive way. If you hold the view that this is the same Mark who is the gospel writer, would he have ever emerged as such without Barnabas? How much of the New Testament would have been different if not for the "grace place" that Barnabas offered. As for Paul, at the end of his life he writes to Timothy with instructions for coming to him and his aide and he tells Timothy to "...Get Mark and bring him with you for he is helpful in my ministry".[13] Seems even the old cold hand of harshness had melted into one of grace.

In dealing with a prodigal, your life needs to be a "grace place". Grace extended is not a condoning of his or her behavior. It is clear understandings of what God could do in someone's life to bring honor to him self. It is not polarizing them but pulling them back into the warmth of companionship. Pride and prejudice stand as major opponents of offering yourself as a "grace place." Pride says you are too good and clean to have such a person around you. Prejudice says that they have in your view gotten away with something and it is your responsibility to make them pay. Neither is correct. Anybody given the right set of circumstances is capable of anything. And for sure God has a way of ensuring that you don't get away with anything.

New Purpose

In my working with men who have been arrested for Domestic Violence cases, God used the limitations there to create restlessness in me. In the process of restoration God begin to stir within me a desire to go further in talking to men. Over a two year period the idea for a ministry aimed primarily at men began to emerge. The more I realized how comfortable my lifestyle had become and that my baggage did not have to be exposed the less I was interested in participating in such a work. However, God continued to stir within me and early in 2003 it became very clear that he was leading in the start of that ministry. In April of 2003 I relinquished my responsibilities with the courts and joined with some other guys in forming a ministry call Servants Alive.

While to date it is in its infancy, we have seen God bring along financial partners who help in the work. We seek to encourage believers to take seriously their walk with God, to embrace the grace of God regardless of the past, and to live their life so they never need restoration. We do conferences, retreats and other ministry opportunities. I am invited to speak frequently to minister's meetings and men's conferences. I am not sure the end result of all of this, but as one who has been to the shed, I can say that wherever He leads, I will go.

Forgotten Grace

There has been an ongoing struggle of dealing with the responses of others. From time to time I encountered people who knew of my past and their response has been to turn and walk away before they reached me. Perhaps they saw me in a store, a restaurant, or other public place and upon seeing me, they quickly leave. There have been more than a few of those encounters and you have to deal with it within yourself and move on.

More difficult has been the response of ministers who have acted as if it was contagious. The experiences have ranged from one who was very close to me before all of this who has refused to extend grace, to those who embrace you as though they had been the prodigal. There have been those to whom I have offered apology and they have forgiven me. Then, there are those who give you a "Judas Kiss" to your face and at the same time work over time to undermine your helping others avoid the same mistakes.

Without question the encouragement has been with those who recognize that "but for the grace of God go I" and put themselves into helping God to continue the restoration process. More than once I have had a minister tell me of his own personal failing that no one else (except the person involved) knew about. The bright eyes of understanding that they have about how bad things could have been for them is refreshing. Wise is the one who recognizes that there are more ways to fail God than just through immorality.

Herein lie's one of the great tensions on the other side of forgiveness. How do you balance the complete, total, embracing forgiveness of God wherein He pronounces you forgiven with the feelings of others that declare you to be a second class Christian? Pity the soul who has forgotten both the need for grace and the burden lifting ability of grace. Pity the one who has reached such a level of spiritual competence that they are now "above" their own baggage of sin.

From time to time I get asked if I have done everything to make it right. In my view I have attempted to do so within the boundaries I now have to work with. For example, I have been asked more than once if I have gone back to my previous congregation to apologize. When it has been made very clear to you that you are not to show up to see your son's baptism, a reasonable person would understand you are not going to have the opportunity to go and stand before the church with an apology. I have taken advantage of chance encounters with members of the church to deal with my failure and to ask for their forgiveness. There are people attached to this carnage that walk away when they are anywhere near you and my understanding is they do not want any conversation with me that would be productive. I understand that and I respect their right to have no further intrusion into their life by me.

I had to come to the place where my negative reaction to people who obviously would not forgive me could be as damaging to me as my prodigal experiences. Sin is sin. I have forgiven and continue to forgive those who cannot accept my personal failure as a learning experience of love and grace. Their attitudes toward me are out of my hands. The only thing I can impact is my attitude toward them. I am growing in my ability to love and forgive them. To do less places me outside the forgiveness of God.

Should the prodigal be transparent? Absolutely! Should there be accountability for one's action? Absolutely! should there be consequences? Yes! Having said such there is nothing that any person or group of people can do to hurt me any greater that the hurt that I brought on myself. Seeking to hold someone's head under the proverbial water as punishment for their sins serves only to bring personal satisfaction to the one holding the head.

¤¤¤¤¤¤¤¤

I am growing in my ability to love and forgive them. To do less places me outside the forgiveness of God.

¤¤¤¤¤¤¤¤

I offer hope and encouragement to any person who has a prodigal in his life. Never give up on him. Never stop praying for him. Never stop loving him.

To the prodigal I say you may not want to talk right now about where you are and what you have become. But there will come a day when you will want to come from the far country that you have found yourself in. Know that there really is a loving heavenly father who has been pursuing you, loving you, and grieving for you; and He stands with arms open and extended ready to embrace you, forgive you, and lead you in the direction of home. Once home with him you will find that he is all about restoration and that he has your best interest at heart. But to return to him you must be willing to come to Him on His terms.

Parents Perspective

There is no doubt to us as parents that Steve came to a place of brokenness. The years following his becoming a prodigal were hard and broke our hearts. Often when we would reach out to him but he would be mean and arrogant contrary to his previous nature. In his chastening he clearly had gone all the way to the bottom.

The years since have proven that he has really repented and come back to the Lord. Blessings have been flowing toward him. In glory we will be able to understand all the unanswered questions. We know that God has been evident in his life. For sure there are nay-sayer's and those who perhaps to this day have great reservations, but that is their problem. We didn't know how to handle this either, but God forgives whether we do or not. He is forgiven notwithstanding the scars that remain.

Things I Wish I could Change

8

As the journey has been pondered there are clearly
things that I wish I could change. While not exhaustive the
list would be inclusive of the following:

The shadow cast on the name of Christ. Basically, it is
immeasurable to see the negative impact done to the cause
of the Savior. How many were disillusioned? How many
discouraged? How many defeated? He lived such a perfect
life. I wish I could take away the shadow cast on Him by
one who claims to follow Him.

*The pain and embarrassment placed on the spouses
and children immediately involved.* None of them were
deserving of what they were forced to face and all of them
were critically wounded. I wish that I could make all of
their grief disappear.

The hurt I caused my parents. The one constant source
of affirmation and rebuke in my life has been two deeply

dedicated parents. I placed them in the position of choosing between their son and God's Son. Even when I did it, I knew who they would choose. They had lived it all their lives. No mother or father should be placed in this position. I wish I could change that but I am so proud they did not waiver. How many bottles does it take to hold their tears? What physical, mental, and emotional impact has it taken on their life? I would heal their heart, dry up all those tears and restore the depleted energy if I could.

The terrible hurt I've caused innocent people. I never dreamed it would be so bad and run so deep. I never dreamed it would stay so long. I know that I will never be fully aware of the total impact on their lives. I would take away the sting of their hurt if I could.

The way my current marriage started. The marriage I live in had such a wrong beginning. Marriages started like mine have two and a half strikes against them from the start. We live with it every day. There is a difference between love and lust. There is a difference between right and wrong. There is a way to start a relationship without creating baggage.

I would change the dark cloud if I could. It ranges from difficulty in understanding why we are still together to can I be trusted again? Earlier I forced others to accept this but it was done out of arrogance. Not it must be accepted because of his grace that he has given us. There is no credibility in running from relationship to relationship. Time alone will answer if I can be trusted. I will tell you that the experience in the shed gives you an incredible clarity as to the cost of disobedience. The dark cloud however, remains.

The damage done to the families involved. There were parents, children, brothers, sisters, grandchildren, and in-laws who have been damaged. For some they are finding the damage so severe that they are struggling to move past it. I wish I could straighten out the damage that has crushed their life.

The scars that I will wear from now on. How many scars do I have? How many would you like to see? There is the scar that comes from destroying a marriage. There is the scar that comes from the loss of credibility. There is the scar that comes from loss of opportunities. There is the scar that is visible from the failure associated with my name. If you look closely you will see scar after scar after scar!

There is one thing that I might have the ability to change; The person who might be in the initial steps of the journey into the prodigal lifestyle. That one, who might read or hear of the horror of the journey and change their mind before taking that first step toward a scarred life; I dedicate my life to helping people avoid the bitter lessons of rebellion I endured. Yes there is grace and forgiveness. Having stated that, what God really desires is for us to get it right to start with. "To obey is better then sacrifice and to heed is better than the fat of rams."[14] If I can help keep one person at home with God and at home with his or her family, perhaps there will be some meaning left for this grace covered prodigal.

Buyer Beware

9

Somewhere in my studies I was told that in the Psalms there is this phrase "Selah" that means to "think about it. Give pause and reflect on the profoundness of what is said. What follows is a consumer tips of buyer beware and "selah" think about from one who has the scars to say buyer beware.

Beware of pride and arrogance
Selah

Beware of playing mind games
Selah

Beware of taking things for granted
Selah

Beware of grass that looks greener
Selah

Beware of responsibilities left undone
Selah

Beware of things you think you can handle
Selah

Beware of consequences you can't control
Selah

Beware of guarding your reputation rather than your heart
Selah

Beware of a loving God who knows no boundaries in
retrieving and restoring you
Selah

Beware of living for the moment
Selah

Beware of thinking your life is yours for the living
Selah

Beware of great potential and lost opportunities
Selah

Beware of burning bridges on dead end streets
Selah

Beware of time stopping for no one
Selah

Beware of a hard head and a cold heart
Selah

Beware of the fact life doesn't come with a rewind button.
Selah

Beware of grace greater than all our sins
Selah

Beware of open manholes and unchecked parachutes
Selah

Beware of slippery slopes and slick bottom shoes
Selah

Beware of the fact that the journey away from the father's
house is easier than the journey back home
Selah

Buyer Beware All Sales Final!
Selah

Prodigal

Like a bird that trails a broken wing
I have come home to Thee;
Home from a flight and freedom
That was never meant for me.

And I, who have known far spaces,
And the fierce heat of the sun,
Ask only the shelter of thy wings,
Now that the day is done

Like a bird that trails a broken wing,
I have come home, at last . . .
O hold me to Thy Heart once more,
And hide me from the past.

Author Unknown

Notes

Chapter 1
1. Proverbs 4:23
2. ICorinthians 10:12
3. Proverbs 16:18

Chapter 2
4. Jeremiah 17:9
5. James 1:17
6. 1 Corinthians 13: 1

Chapter 4
7. Hebrews 12:6
8. 1 Samuel 2:25
9. Luke 22:31
10. Psalms 106: 15

Chapter 5
11. Ephesians

Chapter 7
12. Acts 15: 39
13. 2 Timothy 4:11

Chapter 8
14. 1 Samuel 15:22

Parents Perspective
1. Ruth Graham Bell *Prodigals and Those Who Love Them*
   (Colorado Springs: Focus on the Family Publishing, Colorado 1991),
   p.39
2. Romans 8:28

About the Authors

Stephen Walley is currently the Founder/Director of Servants Alive Ministries. He lives in Daphne Alabama

Gene and Virginia Walley have retired from full time ministry and serve in a part time church. They currently live in their hometown of Richton, Mississippi.

This is the first book for these authors. You may contact them at:

Servants Alive Ministry
122 Donna Circle
Daphne, AL 36525

ServantsAlive@aol.com